W9-DIN-199

Cultural Traditions in
Greece

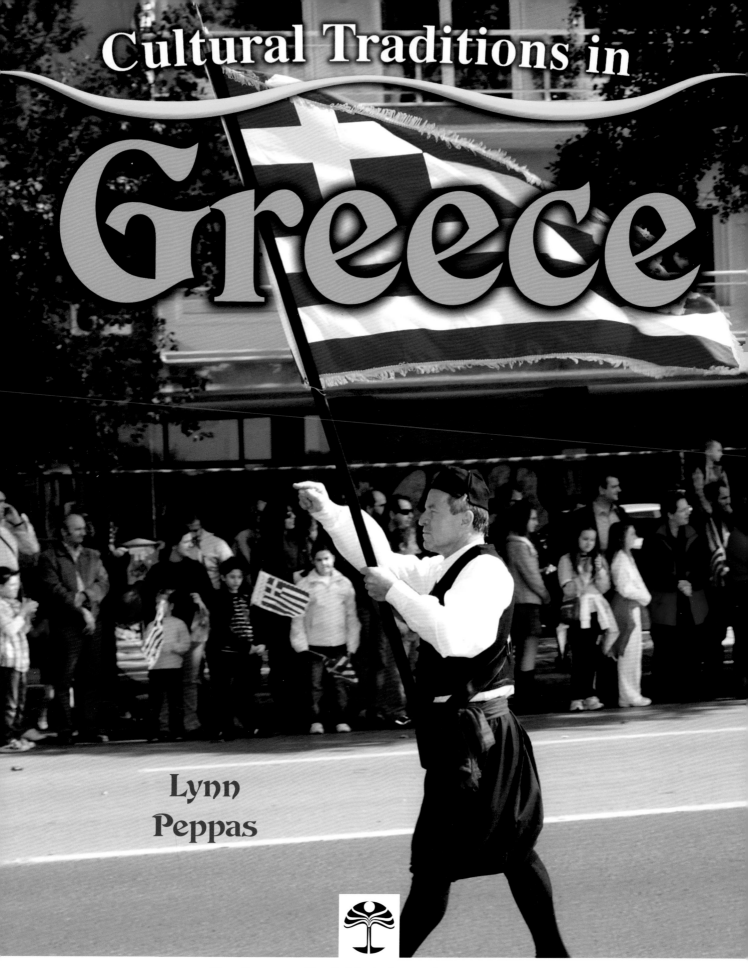

Lynn
Peppas

Crabtree Publishing Company

Crabtree Publishing Company

www.crabtreebooks.com

Author: Lynn Peppas
Publishing plan research and development:
Sean Charlebois, Reagan Miller
Crabtree Publishing Company
Project coordinator: Kathy Middleton
Editors: Adrianna Morganelli, Crystal Sikkens
Photo research: Crystal Sikkens
Design: Margaret Amy Salter
Production coordinator: Margaret Amy Salter
Prepress technician: Margaret Amy Salter
Print coordinator: Katherine Berti

Cover: Syros, a Greek island in the Cyclades, in the Aegean
Sea (background); bougainvillea (top); Venus statue (middle
center); woman in Greek national costume (middle right);
Greek instrument (middle left); ancient Greek dish depicting
Dionysius (bottom left); Baklava (bottom center)

Title page: A participant marches in a National Day
parade in Thessaloniki, Greece.

Photographs:
Alamy: Rebecca Erol: page 6; Terry Harris: pages 8–9;
Percy Ryall: page 25
Associated Press: Dusan Vranic: page 24
iStockphoto: Vasiliki Varvaki: page 19 (bottom right);
Ladida: page 20 (bottom); vasiliki: page 30 (top)
Shutterstock: cover (top, background, bottom center),
pages 4 (except inset), 5, 7 (bottom), 11, 12 (top), 13 (top),
17 (top), 19 (top right), 23, 26 (inset), 27, 29 (top), 31;
AlexTois: title page, page 29 (bottom); C. Cheah : page
4 (inset); Portokalis: pages 14, 15, 17 (bottom), 18–19, 28;
vlas2000: page 26 (except inset)
Thinkstock: cover (except top, background, and bottom
center)
Wikimedia Commons: Kotoviski: page 7 (top); Przykuta:
page 10; Georges Jansoone: page 12 (bottom); Jim Maggas:
page 13 (bottom); Tony Esopi: page 16; Andrzej22: page 19
(middle right); Dimitris Arvanitis: page 20 (top); Kett: page
21; Lemur12: page 22 (top); Jorge-11: page 22 (bottom);
Templar52: page 30 (bottom)

Library and Archives Canada Cataloguing in Publication

Peppas, Lynn
    Cultural traditions in Greece / Lynn Peppas.

(Cultural traditions in my world)
Includes index.
Issued also in electronic format.
ISBN 978-0-7787-7518-8 (bound).--ISBN 978-0-7787-7523-2 (pbk.)

    1. Festivals--Greece--Juvenile literature. 2. Greece--Social
life and customs--Juvenile literature. I. Title. II. Series: Cultural
traditions in my world

GT4851.A2P47 2012   j394.269495   C2012-903962-4

Library of Congress Cataloging-in-Publication Data

Peppas, Lynn.
    Cultural traditions in Greece / Lynn Peppas.
        p. cm. -- (Cultural traditions in my world)
    Includes index.
    ISBN 978-0-7787-7518-8 (reinforced library binding) -- ISBN 978-0-7787-7523-2
(pbk.) -- ISBN 978-1-4271-9042-0 (electronic pdf) -- ISBN 978-1-4271-9096-3
(electronic html)
    1. Festivals--Greece--Juvenile literature. 2. Holidays--Greece--Juvenile
literature. 3. Greece--Social life and customs--Juvenile literature. I. Title.

    GT4851.A2P47 2013
    394.269495--dc23
                                        2012022054

Crabtree Publishing Company

Printed in Canada/102013/MA20130906

www.crabtreebooks.com   1-800-387-7650

Published in Canada
Crabtree Publishing
616 Welland Ave.
St. Catharines, ON
L2M 5V6

Published in the United States
Crabtree Publishing
PMB 59051
350 Fifth Avenue, 59th Floor
New York, New York 10118

Published in the United Kingdom
Crabtree Publishing
Maritime House
Basin Road North, Hove
BN41 1WR

Published in Australia
Crabtree Publishing
3 Charles Street
Coburg North
VIC 3058

Contents

Welcome to Greece

Greece is a country in Europe with a population of almost 11 million people. The country's culture is over six thousand years old. Greek culture has had a great influence on many other cultures around the world. The Greek people celebrate their culture with special holidays and festivals. Some celebrations are thousands of years old and others are very modern.

Athens is the capital city of Greece. It has a population of almost four million people.

Most Greeks follow the Greek Orthodox Christian religion. Christians believe that Jesus Christ is the Son of God. Many public holidays in Greece are based on Christian celebrations.

Did You Know? Every Sunday is a public holiday in Greece by law. Sunday holidays are a very old religious tradition.

Many Greeks celebrate religious holidays throughout the year by attending services at one of the many churches.

Family Occasions

Family is an important part of life in Greece. Ceremonies that celebrate family occasions usually feature the traditional customs of Greek culture. For example, in a Greek Orthodox wedding ceremony, the bride and groom wear wreaths, or crowns, on their heads made of ribbon or beads that are tied together by a ribbon.

Did You Know?
Breaking plates on the floor is an old custom at Greek weddings. In ancient times, it was done to help keep evil spirits away.

The bride and groom are also given a drink of wine in rememberance of Jesus' first miracle where he turned water into wine.

In a Greek Orthodox baptism, the godparent of the baby promises to help the child become a true Christian.

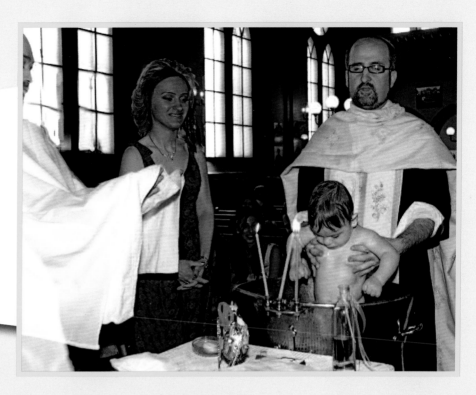

A new baby's baptism is an important religious ceremony for Greek families. During the church service, the priest places the baby carefully in a large bowl of water and olive oil. The priest dunks the baby in the water three times with a blessing or prayer. Family and friends celebrate afterward with a party and a big meal.

At a baptism, olive oil is poured in the bowl of water and rubbed onto the baby's head, hands, and feet.

Name Day

A name day is a religious celebration. Many Greeks are named after saints. A saint is a special, holy person in the Christian Church. Saints have their own special days in the Greek Orthodox Church. On a saint's day, Greeks who are named after the saint celebrate on that day. In the past, a person's name day was more widely celebrated than his or her birthday!

A name day celebration often includes a party and a big meal with friends and family.

On a person's name day, friends and family visit and bring small gifts. Sometimes people celebrating their name day go to a special church service to honor the saint they were named after.

Did You Know?
People with these popular names celebrate their name days on these dates: Nicholas (December 6), Sophia or Sofia (September 17), Michael (November 8), Zoe (December 18), Alexis (March 17), and Alexander (August 30).

New Year's Day

New Year's Day in Greece is on January 1. It is a public holiday when most people get the day off of work or school. New Year's Day is also called St. Basil's Day in Greece. St. Basil was a church leader of the Orthodox Church. He helped poor people.

Did You Know?
January 1 is also
St. Basil's name day.

St. Basil, shown on the left, was a saint known for giving to the needy. Sometimes Greeks give gifts to one another on St. Basil's Day.

On New Year's Day, Greeks bake special bread with a coin inside. The bread or cake is called *vasilopita* in Greek. In English, it is called basil bread. The bread is served during the New Year's Day dinner. The person who finds the coin in their slice of bread will have good luck in the coming year.

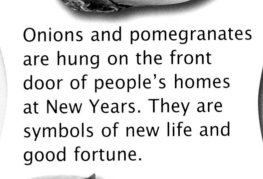

Onions and pomegranates are hung on the front door of people's homes at New Years. They are symbols of new life and good fortune.

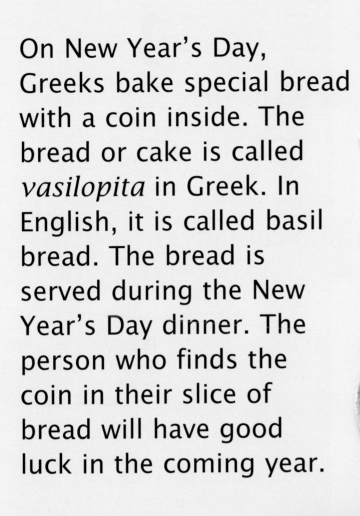

St. Basil gave bread that had coins baked inside to the poor. This way it did not look like charity.

11

Epiphany

Epiphany is a religious holiday in Greece held on January 6. It honors the day that Jesus was baptized by John the Baptist. In Greece, many call this holiday *Fota*, which means "lights" in Greek. Greeks call this holiday the Festival of Lights because on this day Jesus revealed he was the Son of God. Epiphany is a public holiday in Greece.

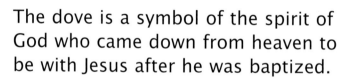

The dove is a symbol of the spirit of God who came down from heaven to be with Jesus after he was baptized.

John the Baptist baptized Jesus in the Jordan River. The Jordan River runs through the modern-day countries of Israel and Jordan.

During Epiphany, worshipers go to special church services. Some churchgoers attend a service at a body of water. This "blessing of the water" service involves the priest throwing a large cross into the water. People then dive into the water to bring the cross back.

Did You Know? During Epiphany, priests bless worshipers' homes by sprinkling water with a basil plant as they walk through different rooms.

The first person to find the cross in the water on Epiphany will enjoy good luck for the rest of the year.

Independence Day

Independence Day is a patriotic holiday in Greece. For a country such as Greece, independence means the freedom to make its own rules. Independence Day is celebrated on March 25. On this day, Greeks remember how the war to win their freedom from Turkish rule began in 1821.

Did You Know?
On Greek Independence Day many schools hold flag parades. Students usually dress in traditional costumes and wave the Greek flag.

Independence Day is a public holiday. Many people attend Independence Day parades that take part in cities throughout Greece.

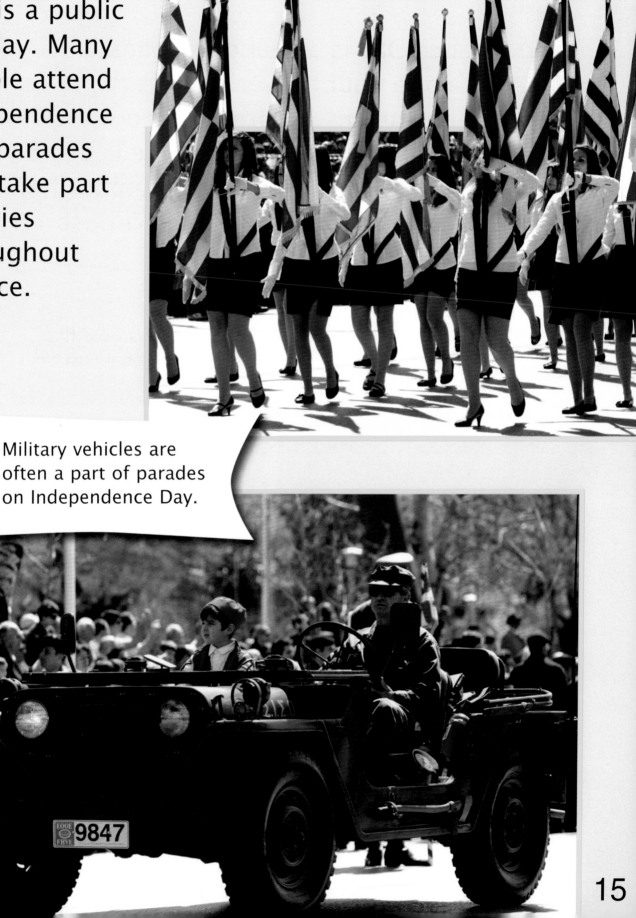

Military vehicles are often a part of parades on Independence Day.

Apokries Festival

Apokries is a time for great fun in Greece. It takes place two weeks before Lent begins. Lent is a religious period of 40 days when Christians do not eat meat or rich foods before Easter. Other Christian cultures celebrate Apokries but call it carnival.

Did You Know? The largest Apokries festival in Greece has been held in the city of Patras for over 150 years. It includes dances, parades, treasure hunts, and fireworks.

Apokries means "goodbye to meat" in Greek. During this time, Greek people enjoy feasts that contain mainly meat before they have to say goodbye to it when the fast begins. People of all ages also have fun singing, dancing, and dressing up in costumes and masks.

Apokries began thousands of years ago in Greece when people held a festival for the pagan Greek god Dionysus.

People dressed in costumes enjoy Apokries festivities in Alexandroupolis, Greece.

Clean Monday

Clean Monday is a religious holiday. It is sometimes called Ash Monday and is the first day of Orthodox Lent. It falls on different dates, but is always 40 days before Easter. It is called Clean Monday because it is a time for a person to clean up, or get rid of, any bad behavior before Easter.

Did You Know? A Clean Monday festive tradition is the flour game. People dump colored flour on top of each other as they parade through the city streets.

Folk dancers perform a traditional dance during Ash Monday celebrations in Thessaloniki, Greece.

In Greece, Clean Monday is a public holiday when most people get the day off work or school. Many fast on this day, and others eat seafood and a special bread called *lagana*. Clean Monday is celebrated in early spring. Many enjoy the tradition of flying kites on this day.

The traditional shape for a kite in Greece is a hexagon—a shape with six sides.

lagana

Easter

Easter is the most important religious holiday in Greece. It falls on different dates within the months of March or April. People in Greece celebrate Easter over four days: Good Friday, Holy Saturday, Easter Sunday, and Easter Monday. Many attend special church services over the Easter holidays. Children are given special three-foot-tall decorated candles to light at church.

On the night of Good Friday, a decorated stand with a sacred image of Jesus (above) is carried through the streets. A procession (below) of members from the church and worshipers in the area follow behind.

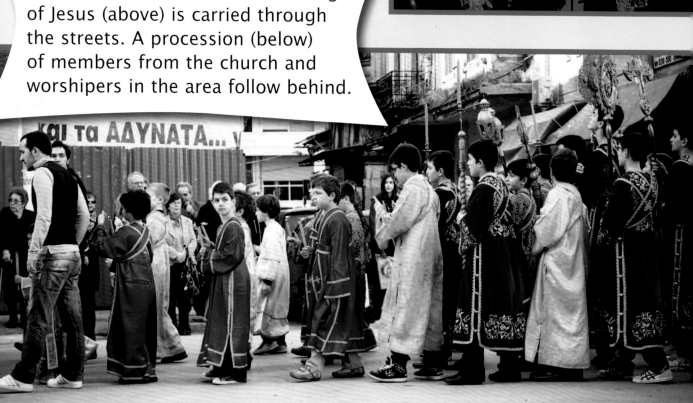

Greek Orthodox Easter only falls on the same dates as the North American Easter once every four years. This is because the North American Easter is based on a different calendar than the one used by the Orthodox Greeks.

In the town of Corfu, it is a tradition to throw pottery from balconies onto the streets on the morning of Holy Saturday.

Easter Sunday

On Easter Sunday, Greek Orthodox Christians celebrate with friends and family. They greet each other saying, *Christos Anesti*. This means "Christ has risen" in English. Families and friends get together to eat a traditional meal of lamb.

Magiritsa is a Greek soup made with lamb. It is eaten on Easter Sunday to break the fast of Lent.

Lamb is often roasted outdoors on a spit, or cooking rod, over an open fire.

Eggs are a popular symbol at Easter time in Greece. Greek Easter eggs are hard-boiled and dyed red in color. People tap the ends of the red eggs together, saying *Christos Anesti.* The person whose egg is not cracked goes on to tap another person's egg. Whoever has the longest-lasting egg will have good luck in the year ahead.

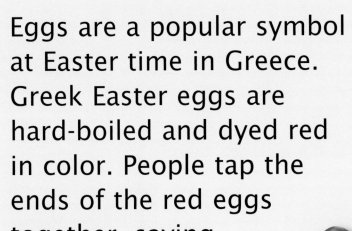

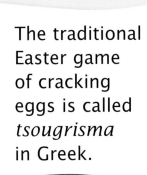

The traditional Easter game of cracking eggs is called *tsougrisma* in Greek.

Assumption Day

Assumption Day is also called the Assumption or Day of the Virgin Mary. Assumption is a religious word that means to go up to Heaven. Assumption Day is a public holiday celebrated on August 15. It is a celebration of the day that Jesus's mother, Mary, went to Heaven.

On the Greek Island of Tinos, thousands of people crawl 2,625 feet (800 meters) on their hands and knees to a church containing an icon of the Virgin Mary. This is done on Assumption Day to show their devotion to Jesus' mother.

Different places in Greece celebrate the Day of the Virgin Mary with dances, feasts, and festivals. Many churches celebrate by carrying an image of Mary through the streets outside the church with churchgoers following behind.

Dancers stand in a circle to perform the Kalamatiano—a popular dance at social events.

Did You Know? Many Greek Orthodox worshipers fast for two weeks before Assumption Day.

Labor Day

Labor Day is celebrated in many countries around the world. It celebrates the many workers in Greece and the hard work they do. In Greece, Labor Day is celebrated on May 1. It is a public holiday, and people enjoy the day off from school or work.

Greece is one of the top ten cotton-producing countries in the world. Inspection workers check the cotton for quality before it is harvested.

People enjoy outdoor activities on Labor Day, such as having a family picnic.

Sometimes Labor Day is called May Day or International Workers' Day. May 1 also marks the Feast of Flowers, a festival honoring spring that was first celebrated thousands of years ago in Greece.

Did You Know?
A tradition on the Feast of Flowers is to pick flowers and make a wreath out of them to hang on your front door.

27

Ochi Day

The Greek word *ochi* (o-hee) means "no." Ochi Day is a patriotic holiday which commemorates the day in 1940 when the Greek people refused to let the Italian army in to occupy their country during World War II.

Greek children often dress in traditional clothing on Ochi Day. The boy in blue and white with a red hat is dressed as an Evzone, which is a special Greek soldier.

Celebrated every year on October 28, people living in Greece get the day off. Many honor their country by hanging the national flag outside their homes. People also enjoy watching parades in large cities such as Athens.

People pay their respects to the soldiers of the Greek army during military parades.

Christmas

Christmas is a religious holiday in Greece. It celebrates Jesus' birthday. It is always celebrated on December 25. Christmas in Greece is a public holiday. The following day, called Boxing Day, is also a holiday.

Decorating Christmas trees is a fairly new Christmas tradition in Greece. Large trees are set up outdoors to decorate cities, such as this one in Athens. Many families also decorate a tree in their own homes.

Decorating for Christmas with a nativity scene is an old tradition in Greece.

Many Greeks who practice the Orthodox religion fast for 40 days before Christmas. On Christmas, families and friends share a big meal of lamb or pork to end the fast. A round, Christmas sweet bread called *Christopsomo*, or Christ bread, is also part of the meal.

Did You Know?
In Greece, St. Nicholas is the patron saint of children. In other cultures, St. Nicholas is sometimes called Santa Claus.

White, sugar-powdered cookies called *kourabiethes* are also eaten at Christmas.

Glossary

behavior The way in which a person acts or behaves

charity Helping people in need

commemorates To act as a reminder of something; to remember or honor

devotion A strong faithfulness or affection toward someone

fast To stop eating all or certain types of food for a period of time

godparent An adult chosen by a child's parents to help raise the child in the Christian faith

national Having to do with a country

nativity scene A scene showing the birth of Jesus

pagan A religion with many different gods usually from ancient times

patriotic A person's pride in his or her country

patron saint A saint believed to guide or protect a person or people

priest A leader of a Christian church that performs religious ceremonies

public The citizens or people who belong to a country

seafood Fish and shellfish that live in the sea

Turkish The culture of people who live in the country of Turkey

worshipers People who show love and devotion to God

Index